A little prayer. . .

which becomes interactive
when the child says the last
line of each prayer.

I see the sun.
The sun sees me.
God bless the sun,
and God bless me.

I see the flowers.
The flowers see me.
God bless the flowers,
and God bless me!

I see the sky.
The sky sees me.
God bless the sky,
and God bless me!

I see the rain.
The rain sees me.
God bless the rain,
and God bless me!

I see the rainbow.
The rainbow sees me.
God bless the rainbow,
and God bless me.

I see the trees.
The trees see me.
God bless the trees,
and God bless me!

I see the snow.
The snow sees me.
God bless the snow,
and God bless me!

I see the robins.
The robins see me.
God bless the robins,
and God bless me.

I see the mountains.
The mountains see me.
God bless the mountains,
and God bless me!

I see the sunset.
The sunset sees me.
God bless the sunset,
and God bless me!

I see the moon.
The moon sees me.
God bless the moon,
and God bless me!

A special thank you to the
anonymous poet
whose four lines of poetry
inspired this little book:

"I see the moon.
The moon sees me.
God bless the moon,
and God bless me."

Made in the USA
Lexington, KY
24 July 2014

Knock Knock Moo Who?

{and other silly animal jokes}

Brenda Ponnay

First Edition
ISBN-13: 978-1-62395-887-9
eISBN: 978-1-62395-888-6
Published in the United States by Xist Publishing
www.xistpublishing.com
PO Box 61593 Irvine, CA 92602

xist Publishing

Knock Knock Moo Who?

{and other silly animal jokes}

Brenda Ponnay

Knock Knock. *Who's There?*
Bow. *Bow who?*

Not Bow who. Bow Wow!

Knock Knock.
Who's There?
Ken.
Ken who?

Ken you walk
the dog for me?

Knock Knock. *Who's There?*
Furry. *Furry who?*

It's your
Furry Godmother.
Hurry up, you're late!

Knock Knock. *Who's There?*
Claw. *Claw who?*

It's Claw Enforcement.
You have the right to remain silent.
Anything you say or do may used against
you in a court of meow.

Knock Knock.
Who's There?
Catsup. *Catsup who?*

Catsup on top of the cupboard
and won't come down!

Knock Knock. *Who's There?*
Purr. *Purr who?*

Purr-fect kitty!

Knock Knock. *Who's There?*
Some bunny. *Some Bunny who?*

Some bunny is eating all my Easter eggs!

Knock Knock. *Who's There?*
Snakeskin. *Snakeskin who?*

Snakeskin bite, but we'd rather run away!

Knock Knock. *Who's There?*
Ssssssssss. *Sssssssss who?*

Make up your mind.
Are you a snake or an owl?

Knock Knock. *Who's There?*
Cows. *Cows who?*

moooooo!

Cows go *moo*! Not who!

Knock Knock. *Who's There?*
Hoo. *Hoo who?*

Hoo!
Hoo!

You talk like an owl!

Knock Knock. *Who's There?*
Goat. *Goat who?*

Goat on a limb and open the door.

Knock Knock. *Who's There?*
Lion. *Lion who?*

Lion on your doorstep. Open up!

Knock Knock. *Who's There?*
Dragon. *Dragon who?*

Dragon your feet again!

Knock Knock. *Who's There?*
Duck. *Duck who?*

Just duck! They're throwing things at us!

Knock Knock. *Who's There?*
Owl. *Owl who?*

Owl Aboard!

Knock Knock. *Who's There?*
Rhino. *Rhino who?*

haha!

Rhino every knock knock joke there is.

Knock Knock. *Who's There?*
Bee. *Bee who?*

Bee at my house at hive o'clock.

Knock Knock. *Who's There?*
Panther! *Panther who?*

Panther no panth, I'm going thwiming!

Knock Knock. *Who's There?*
Amos! *Amos who?*

A mosquito bit me!

Knock Knock. *Who's There?*
Kiwi! *Kiwi who?*

Kiwi go to the store?

Knock Knock. *Who's There?*
Icy! *Icy who?*

Icy a big polar bear up ahead!

Knock Knock. *Who's There?*
Interrupting Cow. *Interrupting...*

Moo!

Knock Knock. *Who's There?*
Monkey! *Monkey Who?*

Monkey see monkey do!

Knock Knock. *Who's There?*
Bach. *Bach who?*

Bach, bach, I'm a chicken!

Knock Knock. *Who's There?*
Tad Pole. *Tadpole who?*

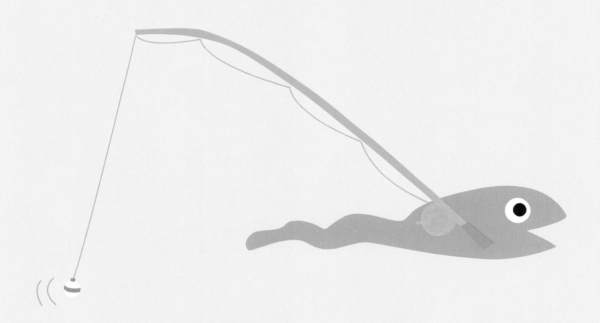

Tad fishing pole is mine!

About the Author

Brenda Ponnay is the author and illustrator of several children's books including the Secret Agent Josephine series: ABC's, Colors and Numbers and the Litle Hoo series. She lives in Southern California with her daughter, who inspires her daily.

You can read all about their adventures on her personal blog www.secret-agent-josephine.com

More Books from Brenda Ponnay

xist Publishing